T0151384

UNHOLY

UNHOLY
DIANE FLACKS

PLAYWRIGHTS CANADA PRESS
TORONTO

For professional or amateur production rights, please contact:
Colin Rivers, Marquis Entertainment
312-73 Richmond St. W., Toronto, ON M5H 4E8
416.960.9123, info@marquisent.ca, www.marquisent.ca

LIBRARY AND ARCHIVES CANADA CATALOGUING IN PUBLICATION
Title: Unholy / Diane Flacks.
Names: Flacks, Diane, author.
Description: A play.
Identifiers: Canadiana (print) 20190153008 | Canadiana (ebook) 20190153016 | ISBN 9780369100276 (softcover) | ISBN 9780369100283 (PDF) | ISBN 9780369100290 (EPUB) | ISBN 9780369100306 (Kindle)
Classification: LCC PS8561.L264 U54 2019 | DDC C812/.6—dc23

Playwrights Canada Press acknowledges that we operate on land, which, for thousands of years, has been the traditional territories of the Mississaugas of the Credit, Huron-Wendat, Anishinaabe, Métis, and Haudenosaunee peoples. Today, this meeting place is home to many Indigenous peoples from across Turtle Island and we are grateful to have the opportunity to work and play here.

We acknowledge the financial support of the Canada Council for the Arts—which last year invested $153 million to bring the arts to Canadians throughout the country—the Ontario Arts Council (OAC), Ontario Creates, and the Government of Canada for our publishing activities.

To my parents, Lily and Cy Flacks, who sent me to thirteen years of Hebrew school and worried that it might have been a waste. To my children, Eli and Jonny Purdy-Flacks, whose questions launched me toward this play. To Janis Purdy, who championed my creative deep dives through the years, and to Tommie-Amber Pirie, who answered the question, "If not god, then what do we worship?"

PREFACE

Life imitates art imitates life. When I approached Kelly Thornton, then artistic director of Nightwood Theatre, about the idea of a play about misogyny and religion set in a debate, I couldn't have dreamt up Trump's Muslim ban, the Quebec mosque and Pittsburgh synagogue shootings, Brett Kavanaugh or #MeToo. I wanted to write a play about subjects that consumed and outraged me since a rabbi refused to shake my hand at Hebrew school and since my own children started asking pointed questions about god, love, suffering and violence. By the time *Unholy* premiered in 2017, the intersection of misogyny and religion had become hauntingly present in all our lives. The theatre allowed us all a space to talk. Now, the issues have become even more pressing and, at times, surreal. Hearing and questioning each other's perspectives, especially those you can't comprehend, and with which you deeply disagree, is even more vital a task today. The forces of misogyny are even more in need of confrontation than before. I am so grateful to have the chance to do so with the publication of *Unholy*.

The choice of a debate as a framework for the play was inspired by a groundbreaking 1989 NFB film about women and faith called *Half the Kingdom*. The documentary's synopsis says, "Seven women strive to find common ground between religious and cultural tradition and contemporary feminist principles." Ten years after this documentary was made, in 1999, a live "reunion" debate was held in Toronto with most of the original participants. I was there that night and was captivated by the struggle that many of these women faced trying to justify to us and to each other why they still held to their religious beliefs. Especially intriguing was the ability to live in apparent cognitive dissonance—as a feminist and a religious person.

Ultimately, *Unholy* is about the "biblical" struggles that tear us apart personally and tribally, and that make us who we are. It's about having the courage to leap in life and into love. What is more holy than that?

I am grateful for the deep personal and professional commitment of Kelly and Nightwood Theatre, Colin Rivers, and all the incredible actors and artists who've participated in each of the productions and workshops. This stuff is not easy to wrestle with or share, and that's why I believe we should.

—Diane Flacks, August 2019

A workshop production of *Unholy* was first presented in fall 2015 as part of Nightwood Theatre's New Groundswell Festival of contemporary women's theatre, presented at Buddies in Bad Times Theatre, Toronto.

The play made its world premiere January 15–29, 2017, in a production by Nightwood Theatre at Buddies in Bad Times Theatre, with the following cast and creative team:

Liz Feldman-Grant: Diane Flacks
Maryam Al Hashemi: Bahareh Yaraghi
Yehudit and Lucy: Niki Landau
Sister Margaret and Sadie: Barbara Gordon
Richard: Blair Williams

Director: Kelly Thornton
Lighting Design: Bonnie Beecher
Set and Costume Design: Lindsay C. Walker
Composer and Sound Design: Richard Feren
Projection Design: Laura Warren
Movement Direction: Viv Moore
Stage Manager: Christina Cicko
Assistant Director: Sadie Epstein-Fine
Wardrobe Coordinator: Christine Urquhart
Managing Director and Producer for Nightwood Theatre: Beth Brown

The premiere was extended due to popular demand until February 5, 2017, and the show was subsequently honoured with a 2017 Dora Mavor Moore Award nomination for Outstanding New Play.

Nightwood was proud to present a return engagement of *Unholy* as part of its 2017/18 season, from November 23 to December 10, 2017, at Buddies in Bad Times. Nightwood later partnered with Consulting Producer for Nightwood Theatre Colin Rivers and ZoomerMedia for a VisionTV special to share the piece with a live TV studio audience for the very first time November 16–18, 2018.

CHARACTERS

Liz Feldman-Grant
Maryam Al Hashemi
Yehudit Kalb
Lucy
Sister Margaret Donaghue
Sadie
Richard

NOTES

A forward slash (/) indicates where the characters' speeches over-lap, except in the opening scene, where the characters speak over top of each other at once.

The stage is set up for a debate with two teams. There are four comfortable chairs, situated behind two tables, and a podium in the centre. The chairs all have mics.

A slide at the back of the stage reads, "Should Women Abandon Religion? A Unique Ideas Now Debate, with your host: Richard Morris."

At the downstage is a long, low narrow beam.

There are four panellists on stage. On one side is MARYAM, a poised young lawyer wearing a light silk scarf around her neck, and YEHUDIT, a confident Orthodox Jewish scholar in her late thirties to early forties. On the other side is LIZ, a middle-aged antitheist, stylishly dressed, and MARGARET, an ex-nun in her seventies.

At a podium is the moderator, RICHARD, smooth, charming, smarter than he looks.

Lights snap up on the debate. They are mid-fight, all loudly talking at once, concurrently, overlapping. The debate is played realistically—the women listening and taking notes and fighting for their points.

MARYAM: No no no wait wait wait—

LIZ: Answer the question—

MARYAM: Listen, listen—

YEHUDIT: UnbeLIEvable!

RICHARD: One at a time! One at a time.

LIZ: I'm simply asking—

MARGARET: Richard . . . Can we . . . oh my . . .

YEHUDIT: OutRAgeous!

LIZ: Wow, this is—

MARYAM: I'm trying to—

RICHARD: All right all right all right! One at a time! Ladies ladies! MICS!

> *RICHARD motions to the booth to cut off the women's mics, which they do. For a minute, everyone is still arguing with less sound.*

(*to audience*) That was Dominic. Give us a flash, Dominic.

> *The stage lights flash.*

Dominic is our floor director. He's the grand overseer of the five TV cameras that are recording this debate tonight for our YouTube channel. He swears this debate will help us break one million views and I tip my hat to that. Now, ladies, ladies, ladies, we appreciate your passion, believe me, and I did promise a brief free discussion before your opening statements, but free does not mean yelling. We have to at least be able to hear / each other—

LIZ starts talking, despite her mic being off. After a beat, RICHARD motions for it to be restored.

LIZ: What *I* hear, with respect, are apologists. Look, Richard, I want to say that every religion has at its core a hard and polished gem of beauty. I want to say that the goal of religion is to bring love and compassion to this sadistic and lonely world. I want to say that . . . But I can't. Because it's not true. In Tennessee, a bill was voted into law almost unanimously, and it's one of a wave of these bills eviscerating the US—in this handmaid's-tale dystopian deathly reality show we are living in—but this one is for *schools*: the Religious Viewpoints Anti-Discrimination Act. Sounds *affirming*, right? Like "men's rights"? Or "REAL Women" or "alt-right"? Or "populist."

Well, it would allow homophobic kids to physically assault gay kids in the name of freedom of religious expression. This is happening now.

YEHUDIT: Exactly. In the *name* of religion. Religion is being *used*. I can't speak for the alt-right Christians, but in Orthodox Judaism this is not acceptable. A key tenet is *Kvod HaBriyot*, *respect* for all creations, for human / dignity.

LIZ: *This* is happening now, in the name of our religion: in Jerusalem, an eight-year-old girl is surrounded and spat on by a group of bearded, sweating *Haredi* men for "dressing immodestly." She's eight! She should be able to dress like a unicorn if she wants to!

RICHARD laughs.

Or a TV host. Journalist?

RICHARD: Ya.

LIZ: Ya. *This* is happening now: ISIS, ISIL, whatever, are—

MARYAM: We prefer "Daesh," which is pejorative.

LIZ: You don't want to talk about ISIS, can we talk about Boko Haram, then? Which translates as "education is forbidden," if I'm not mistaken, Maryam?

MARYAM: I don't speak Arabic. I'm Iranian. I speak Farsi. / As you know.

LIZ: Do you? Remember those two hundred girls who were kidnapped in Nigeria four years ago? We had to forget about them in the face of the next atrocity perpetrated in the name of Islam. Boko Haram is now using girls as walking explosives, / as human bombs—

MARYAM: Boko Haram do not represent Islam. The prophet Mohammad, upon him be peace, said the opposite, "seek education from the cradle to the grave."

LIZ: And if you're a Muslim girl, seeking education can get you shot in the face.

RICHARD: Margaret—you believe that women should abandon the Catholic Church?

MARGARET: Well, yes.

RICHARD: You have left the Catholic Church.

MARGARET: Yes. I am an ex-nun. I've just got my one-year chip.

RICHARD: Really?

MARGARET: No. I'm making a joke about Alcoholics Anonymous.

RICHARD: But you still refer to yourself as a Catholic. You're not an *ex*-Catholic.

MARGARET: If Jesus were walking around now, seeing how the Catholic Church has betrayed his message, simply, of love and compassion, he would just . . . shake the rafters! The Catholic Church needs to own up to the damage they have done and beg for forgiveness—

RICHARD: Would you forgive them?

MARGARET: Well, I'd like to see it happen.

YEHUDIT: *Some* things are unforgivable.

RICHARD catches this and presses her.

RICHARD: So, Yehudit—

He pronounces her name incorrectly, like Yehoodiht.

—no forgiveness for sin?

YEHUDIT: Jews are not so much into forgiveness. It's Yehu*deet*.

RICHARD: (*trying, failing*) Yehudiht?

LIZ: It's true. Forgiveness and Jews? Not so much.

YEHUDIT: It is a little namby-pamby. "I'm sorry, I did it" and it's over? No. You need to make restitution, take action. We say "*teshuvah*," turning all the way around.

RICHARD: Pope John Paul apologized in 2000—

MARGARET: He did. Oh he was a lovely, lovely pope. For the Crusades, the Inquisition, the persecution of the Jews, uh, (*reading from her notes*) let me just . . . see . . . the silence during the Holocaust, the oppression of women, the forced conversion of Indigenous people, limbo—that was a cruel mistake and he admitted it. I had high hopes after that, but it went the other way.

RICHARD: Pope Francis said gay people are welcome—

LIZ: And so are pedophiles. Come on. Friendly Francis? It's a sham. And he clearly isn't welcoming women into the tent—

MARGARET: No women clergy.

LIZ: Which / would change—

MARGARET: Which would change everything. Sorry, Liz, / go ahead.

LIZ: Go ahead.

MARGARET: You— /

LIZ: No, you. / Go.

MARGARET: Go. You . . . Uhhhh . . . ?

    MARGARET has lost her train of thought.

LIZ: (*prompting*) No women clergy . . . which is . . .

MARGARET: Right, because *then* the Catholic Church would have to take children and families really into account in all their / actions.

LIZ: Instead we have a bunch of celibate men in dresses with their vaginal-probe population police telling Catholics how to have families. When do we say enough?!

MARYAM: Rabbah Yehudit and I are saying it every day, and we don't have to cut off our noses to spite our faces. My opponent's complaint is with fundamentalism. Fundamentalism—in religions, as in secular politics—is an immature fear-based response. I'm confident that, with thought, with honesty and guidance, religion will grow out of it. And my question is: What will we grow into? Cynicism, more fear, isolationism?

LIZ: Cynicism is healthy.

YEHUDIT: Cynicism is easy.

MARYAM: You say you cannot be a feminist and believe in religion? Well, here I am.

> *MARYAM steps out of her chair and strides forward confidently toward the audience. Then she turns toward LIZ and holds out her hand for LIZ to touch. It is a provocative and vulnerable gesture. LIZ is uncomfortable but does it. MARYAM holds LIZ's hands affectionately.*

See, you can touch me and neither of us dissolve.

> *MARYAM kisses MARGARET on her cheeks. MARGARET adores it. She whispers to LIZ, accidentally speaking fully into her mic.*

MARGARET: She's a lovely girl.

MARYAM smiles and addresses the audience.

MARYAM: I know when you first came in here tonight, you voted for which team you think should win, and I expect, Yehudit, that we are the underdogs in this crowd. Yes, Richard?

RICHARD: According to these first vote results, I'm going to have to say yes, but the audience will vote again at the end. The winner of this debate will be the team who changes the most minds.

MARYAM: Wonderful.

YEHUDIT: *Baruch HaShem. [God bless.]*

MARYAM: So. I ask you to contemplate this: women multi-task, yes? We can hold duality of thought, two seemingly opposing ideas at once: life and death, joy and rage—or as I do: feminism and religion. As my learned colleague Rabbah Yehudit says, religion is not the cause of evil. It's our attitude toward it that determines whether we choose to be united in the light, or divided in the dark.

LIZ: What's more divisive than religion?

YEHUDIT: Politics, money—

MARYAM: Race, sex—

YEHUDIT: Power—

MARYAM: Narcissism.

LIZ: And of all these, religion is the worst.

YEHUDIT: Judaism *honours* women.

LIZ: As child-bearing machines, right, Margaret?

MARGARET: Right. Oh, / wrong.

MARYAM: In Islam, a mother must be shown three times the kindness of anyone else. The prophet Mohammad, upon him be peace, when asked who should be shown the most compassion, said, "Your mother." Who next? "Your mother." Who / next—

LIZ: Mohammad married a nine-year-old girl.

MARYAM: That was in the context of his time. People only lived to forty-five—

LIZ: Tell that to Roy Moore. In 2014, an eleven-year-old Muslim child bride died in Yemen, her pelvis broken on her wedding night / by her forty-year-old husband—

MARYAM: This is an apocryphal story. / Google it.

LIZ: Sure, why listen to girl victims?

MARYAM: The Quran *commands* us to speak against evils like this. "Believers conduct yourself with justice and bear true witness before god, even if it be against yourselves, your parents, and your community."

LIZ: And a female witness is worth one half of a man.

MARYAM: Richard, I am—

(*to* YEHUDIT) *We* are—going to build something, not just tear down. My new progressive Muslim movement calls for real Islam: peace.

LIZ: You were the one who received death threats—

MARYAM: And I am not afraid! If we can allow the best of religious values to inspire us to be our best selves, exclude no one in doing so, we women will change the world! In the words of the late Czech president Václav Havel, "The rules of human coexistence can work only if they grow out of the deepest experience of *everyone*, not just some."

RICHARD: Here we go!

> *RICHARD claps his hands together, excited—the game is on. Lights.*

> *Transition.*

> *The women walk to the downstage edge of the stage and go into individual moments of "prayer" or holiness under music. YEHUDIT prays with a talit; MARGARET does her rosary; MARYAM washes her hands and arms, then kneels and begins to pray; and LIZ scrolls through her phone and chuckles.*

> *Then the ding of elevator doors opening and the four walk in. It is the night before the debate. They are in the elevator together for a moment.*

THE ELEVATOR

YEHUDIT: Good night.

MARGARET: See you tomorrow.

MARYAM: See you in the morning.

> *MARGARET and YEHUDIT leave. LIZ and MARYAM stand in the elevator. Beat.*

LIZ: Are you on eighteen?

MARYAM: Seventeen.

LIZ presses the button for MARYAM's floor.

Thanks.

LIZ: Mmhm.

Pause. LIZ looks at her phone.

MARYAM: Well, that was a fun dinner.

LIZ: Was it?

Beat.

Listen, they don't usually give you dinner the night before these debates. Much less put you up in a hotel.

MARYAM: But you didn't seem to like the food.

LIZ: It tried too hard. It was like a bad joke: What do you make for dinner for an Orthodox Jew, a Muslim and a Catholic septuagenarian diabetic?

MARYAM: Chicken.

LIZ: Exactly.

MARYAM: And you sent it back—

LIZ: Well, it was dry.

MARYAM: What do you make for an atheist Jewish perfectionist?

LIZ: The chicken wasn't dry? Please, the whole thing was meh.

MARYAM: I would never say meh.

LIZ: And that's how I'll beat you in the debate tomorrow, my dear. You're thinking it. I'll say it. The chicken was beyond meh, it was meh exponential, the hyperbolic plateau of mediocre meh-ness. If you don't think that was meh, I do not know what is.

MARYAM: Okay, you win. The chicken was meh.

LIZ: But the rice was fantastic.

LIZ smiles at her own joke. MARYAM peruses her.

MARYAM: You're more likeable in person.

LIZ: . . . Thanks?

MARYAM: Seriously, you should think about that for tomorrow.

LIZ: Oh I will.

MARYAM: You're not as arrogant in person.

LIZ: And you are not nearly as insufferably self-righteous as you are on your website.

MARYAM: Just wait.

LIZ: Forewarned.

Beat. MARYAM still peruses LIZ.

MARYAM: And you're shorter. On your VisionTV series, you came off as—tall, and humourless.

LIZ: Oh *you* were the one person who watched that show.

MARYAM: When I was a teenager. In my parents' basement. Secretly.

LIZ: Your parents didn't approve?

MARYAM: Oh no.

LIZ: Do they approve of you now?

MARYAM: Well . . . My father does.

LIZ: Your mother?

MARYAM: She worries.

LIZ: For your safety?

MARYAM: My marriageability.

LIZ: But you don't?

MARYAM: I'm too busy.

LIZ: Congratulations. You're igniting a movement.

MARYAM: I can only hope to have as great a legacy as you have.

LIZ: "Legacy"? That makes me feel a hundred.

MARYAM: Not at all! I hope that I will look as good as you do when I'm your age.

Awkward beat. The elevator door opens.

Do you want to have a drink?

LIZ: Thank you, but I think I better prepare for you tomorrow.

MARYAM: I was given some lovely wine at my book signing yesterday. I shouldn't drink it alone.

MARYAM leaves.

LIZ hesitates.

Lights.

THE DEBATE

LIZ moves to the podium. On the screen upstage, there is a posed 8" × 10" picture of her (from younger days). Under the photo it says, "Liz Feldman-Grant, internationally recognized speaker and author of A Genocidal God, *winner of the RBC Taylor Prize for non-fiction."*

RICHARD: She's an author, a pundit and a provocateur, please welcome our first speaker, Liz Feldman-Grant. You will have two minutes, Liz, and then we'll move on to a speaker from the other side. Then the panellists will have time to comment.

(to audience) Everyone, keep an open mind.

LIZ speaks to the audience, the cameras and her fellow panellists. The panellists react and take notes.

LIZ: Thank you. I will say what many of you are thinking: "Couldn't you just lay off god, Liz? It's *organized religion* that is all greedy and misogynist and hateful and terrified and controlling." True.

But, with respect, that's a cop out. If we take god *out* of organized religion, it loses its power. Saying "god" allows individuals to behave like god—like an inhuman, genocidal maniac, mostly toward women.

Take god out of religion, and you know what you're left with? Cute campy cultures that can't hurt anyone. "Wow, there's a saint for losing your keys. That is adorable, but non-threatening." Now let's go back to our real lives, with our real consequences to our real, human moral codes and behaviours. Our inherent human morality is more just, more compassionate, more effective than anything these reward- and punishment-based systems of control have dreamt up. Think about this: god is love, but we have to fear god. So I put to *you*, my esteemed colleagues, we cannot love each other without it being poisoned a little bit by fear. That's why we are divided today.

With respect, if you are a feminist—and, let's face it, you are—you *must* abandon religion *and* whichever god fuels it, because even if you *quietly* support a system that allows priests to rape little boys, or imams to lock girls in their dark houses until they dissolve from lack of vitamin D, or rabbis to painstakingly check the vaginal secretions of everyone's mother and sister, you are as culpable as they are. You *know*. You know that disease is caused by germs and not by sin, and that agreeing to dominate and silence half the world's population has been an utter, evil failure. And we *cannot* know any more and do nothing. There is no more middle ground in this low-rent Gilead.

And what about personal faith? I guess you can have your faith; I have my tequila. But really, how does god help you deal with suffering any better than carrot soup and two really good friends? Really?

Why do you have faith? Because you grew up with it? Well, I grew up with it, but then I grew up. The story goes that the people said to god, "We need help, why don't you send someone!" And god answered, "I did, genius. I sent you." We are it. We are enough. And we have had enough! Face it. Say it. It's enough! Religion needs to get ten feet the hell away from women's bodies and souls! You know it, you have had it and now—really, if not now, my friends, then when— for your daughters, for your sons, for our planet, for each other, you must say it! And you can. Now. With your votes. Thank you.

RICHARD: (*applauding*) Thank you, Liz.

> *LIZ looks at MARYAM. MARYAM looks back.*

> *LIZ sits. MARGARET pats her hand. They confer and write notes as RICHARD speaks.*

Maryam? You are a Muslim.

MARYAM: Go on.

RICHARD: And you're a lawyer, and a women's advocate, and the youngest member of the Law Society's women's justice association. This seems complicated to me.

MARYAM: I will make that easier for you. In a nutshell: we both may not like that a woman must wear the niqab in public in Saudi Arabia, but while you would abandon her, I would embrace her.

RICHARD: You have two minutes.

> *MARYAM addresses the audience. On the screen behind her we see a current, glam picture of MARYAM and the bio: "Maryam Hashemi, lawyer, co-founder of Modern Islam Now Equitably (MINE) and co-chair of the Ontario Islamic Women's Legal Circle."*

MARYAM: I am a modern Canadian Iranian woman. I choose my occupation, my intimate partners, and *at the same time*, like my esteemed colleague Rabbah Yehudit, I receive joy from my family, culture and my god. I would not be *me* without them, and—

(*to LIZ*) "With respect," I will not sacrifice them to the idol of ideology. When my family came here from Iran in the late nineties, we were embraced by the Canadian Muslim community. As a young girl, if anyone bullied me at school, I had six big cousins, with three eyebrows between them, to watch my back.

(*to LIZ*) I feel deeply sad that you think worshipping god brings fear and tyranny. When I pray to my god, I feel love and peace.

Yes, absolutely, there is a problem in many Islamist states, who are hijacking and corrupting Islam for their own power. Some would say the feminist movement has been hijacked too, by the strident . . . But contrary to some of the mischaracterizations of Islam that many in the West find convenient to perpetuate, the Quran famously states that whoever kills one person, it's as if they killed all of humanity; whoever saves a life, saves the world.

And I must ask: Has secularism done better? Stalin, the Cultural Revolution, Hitler? Trump?? Fascism, very alive and well, is based not on religion but, arguably, on race. Should we therefore abandon *race*, or does diversity not make us all more beautiful?

May I quickly quote my second favourite atheist Jew, after our friend, Liz? This is from Charlie Chaplin from his film *The Great Dictator*.

YEHUDIT nods and smiles at the Charlie Chaplin reference.

Dressed reminiscently of Hitler, he makes a speech to an auditorium full of soldiers.

"Our knowledge has made us cynical. Our cleverness, hard and unkind. We think too much and feel too little. More than machinery we need humanity. More than cleverness we need kindness and gentleness. Without these qualities, life will be violent and all will be lost."

If I had a vote tonight, I would vote for the fullness of the heart, not the head. If we dive into religion, instead of rejecting it, it will nourish all of our hearts. Of that, we can never have "enough." Thank you.

MARYAM *looks at* LIZ.

RICHARD: Thank you, / Maryam—

LIZ: May I just say, I am a big fan of youth engagement and leadership. Congratulations. I applaud your courage in being here, in the lion's den. You too, Yehudit.

YEHUDIT: "Courage"? We are all mature women sitting here having a thoughtful YouTube discussion. *Nu?* "Lion's den"? Come on, Liz. You want to scare us? Try harder. Please. *Shoin. [Enough.]* "Courage"? What's going to happen?

Lights focus on YEHUDIT.

Music. "Od Y'shama." Jewish wedding music. It's something only YEHUDIT *hears. Now* YEHUDIT *smiles, but it's* YEHUDIT *from fifteen years ago.*

YEHUDIT'S SISTER'S WEDDING

YEHUDIT's had a bit to drink. She has a big swig of wine and jumps up and down to the music. YEHUDIT sings the last refrain, "Od Yishama b'Arei Yehudah Uv'chutzot Yerushalayim Kol sason v'kol simcha Kol chatan v'kol kalah!" Then she yells into the microphone.

YEHUDIT: Wooooooo! *Sheket! [Quiet!] Behvakashah . . . [Please . . .]*

The music quiets on the women's side of the wedding. YEHUDIT's mother, her emah, SADIE, in her fifties, sits to the side watching and reacting. She's overheated but full of nachus [joy]. She is played by the actress playing MARGARET.

I want to say a few words about the bride, my big sister, Leah, the most kind, loyal sister anyone could ask for. Is Surrahleh Zaretsky here? It wasn't Leah that broke your nose with the yo-yo at Camp Mossad, it was me! Leah took the blame. That's the kind of person she is. Leah, I will miss your gentle voice and the bossy notes you leave in the mornings about the dog's thyroid medication. Ezra had better treat you like the queen you are.

(calls off stage) You hear that, Ezra?

(back to the audience) Do you think they could hear that over on the men's side?

She giggles and raises her drink.

To Leah and Ezra! Whoooo! *L'Chaim!*

As you know, every family has its roles, and in our family, Leah is the beauty, I am the brains! So, let me talk Torah for a minute. You know I love the *parshahs* about family in the Torah. But when you find yourself a character in them—when you're Jacob wrestling with your angel or Rebecca bursting with twins in a hot tent, pinned under their weight, hearing the voice of an angel saying, "You're going to like one child better and you'll help him cheat the other of his birthright, to become Hashem's chosen," yikes!

She points to her mom and laughs.

Emaaaah! Or you're Leah, who got married to Jacob by trickery when he really preferred her younger sister, Rachel.

The music and underlying party chit-chat completely clink clank clanks to a stop.

And then you don't feel alone because you've been studying it all your life and you know it's so true! And sad and Hashem feels so bad for us that we have to go through this stuff—and—and—Leah and Ezra! *L'Chaim!*

SADIE gets the music to start up again.

No, no wait, one more thing.

The music stops.

The day after tomorrow, I'm going to *Eretz Yizroel* to study in Jerusalem! To leap into a whole new life!! It's the new millennium, the year 2000, according to the common era, and President Bill Clinton and Ehud Barak and Yasser Arafat—

She reacts to audience booing.

I know, I know, the PLO never misses an opportunity to miss an opportunity—they are meeting in Camp David. Maybe there will be peace in the Middle East! And maybe Leah and Ezra will be happy!

To Leah and Ezra! Unbelievable! *L'Chaim!*

YEHUDIT over-cheers and stumbles. Lights. Facing the audience, young YEHUDIT subtly ages into the substantial woman she is today, her hair covered and tucked under a cap, her youth dissipated. The debate music abruptly starts again. Lights shift.

THE DEBATE

MARGARET is in mid-comment.

MARGARET: I love the Jews, I do.

LIZ: That makes one of us.

RICHARD: Would you call yourself a self-loathing Jew, Liz?

LIZ: I am a culinary Jew.

YEHUDIT: *(guffaws)* Ha. There is a long tradition of angry Jewish atheists, Richard.

MARYAM: Anger comes from fear.

LIZ: Or anger.

YEHUDIT: It's one of my life missions to reach people like you, Liz.

LIZ: I hope you don't smoke.

RICHARD: Margaret, / you had a point about—

LIZ: 'Cause you'll need a long life / to achieve that mission—

YEHUDIT: I got it, yes, smoking— /

LIZ: Smoking. Yes.

MARGARET: —yes, a point about the Jews, yes.

RICHARD: Well, we have just another minute for comments. Margaret.

MARGARET: Yes, well, what I don't like, Yehudit, is this I can't shake a man's hand business. That happened to me and it was explained that the men are afraid a woman is on her period and that that's unclean.

YEHUDIT: Well, they're not unclean as in impure or shameful. They're "*tameh.*"

MARGARET: Which means . . . ?

YEHUDIT: Well, it doesn't mean sinful. We don't endorse the Catholic notion of original sin.

MARGARET: But it means . . . ?

YEHUDIT: *Tameh* means the opposite of holy—

LIZ: MUCH better.

YEHUDIT: —in terms of *life and death*. When someone comes in contact with death, like the death of an ovum, or blood, or in biblical times an animal, we take a *moment*, to *stop*, to be *still*, and mark the holiness of all life. As Maryam does in prayer. *Nidah*, that one week in a woman's cycle, is a beautiful time, and like Shabbat, if you follow it, it can bring a couple *closer*.

LIZ: Love it.

YEHUDIT: When a woman is separated from her husband during *Nidah*, she rests, with other women—don't you all wish to do that when you're on your period—sorry, Richard—

RICHARD: You don't have to apologize to me. Period. Big deal. Menstruation.

A beat as the women all look at him.

Go on.

YEHUDIT: In that time, her husband misses her. If I can be honest, when you can touch again, the sex is great. Because it's been forbidden.

LIZ: Were you *shomreh negiya* before you were married?

RICHARD: What is that?

YEHUDIT: A male and female couple can't touch before they are married.

LIZ: Did you have an arranged marriage?

YEHUDIT: I did. Most of my secular friends are on their third divorce. It works.

LIZ: Don't you think you are worth more than "working"?

YEHUDIT: What, you think Tinder is a better way to meet your future spouse?

LIZ: Unlike my colleague (*referring to* MARYAM), I'm not looking to get married, thank you for your concern though. So, according to this archaic, made-up, property-based code that you've devoted your life to, you're forbidden to touch before you marry, and then once you're married, you can't touch when you're on your period.

YEHUDIT: (*to* MARYAM) You think maybe she's a little obsessed with touching?

LIZ: I understand your husband wasn't allowed to touch you when you were giving *birth*.

YEHUDIT: My mother was there. My sister, Leah, was there. That's who I wanted—Richard, I am not going to talk about my family. Okay?

RICHARD: Um, sure.

YEHUDIT: Please. Some respect. Honestly.

RICHARD: Okay. Yes—

YEHUDIT: We are not delving into anyone else's personal life—

LIZ: Our side is an open book, right, Margaret? Ask away!

MARGARET: Well, if I may, I don't really see how Yehudit's intimate relationship with her husband is relevant to the debate.

LIZ is surprised by that.

YEHUDIT: Thank you. Honestly.

MARYAM: Honestly, Liz.

MARGARET: Although, in my experience, working in a Catholic hospital for twenty-seven years, it is best for a husband to be at the birth of his child. Scar him for life!

MARGARET tries to pat LIZ's arm, but LIZ shifts away.

RICHARD: That's true. When my wife pushed, the wall behind me looked like a Jackson Pollock painting. That's bravery!

He laughs.

All right, can we move on?

YEHUDIT: Please.

RICHARD: Margaret—this is your first televised debate, isn't it?

MARGARET: Oh, yes it is.

RICHARD: Well, you are a brave woman for being here and speaking out. At your age. At any age! I think we can all agree on that.

MARGARET: Oh no, no.

RICHARD starts to applaud her.

RICHARD: Come on now—we all agree. Thank you so much.

MARGARET: No. No.

He applauds her, as do the other panellists, and she is embarrassed by the applause. She backs away from it, in effect backing into her memory.

Transition.

We hear ambient hospital sounds, announcements. The sounds of rubber shoes squeaking down a hallway. Under this MARGARET *has become herself about ten years ago. She wears her habit. She is waiting for a guest. She's nervous.*

The actor playing YEHUDIT *has become* LUCY, *a young street-involved kid, with heavy-duty boots, a toque and lots of 'tude.*

MARGARET'S OFFICE AT THE CATHOLIC HOSPITAL

LUCY: Got anything to drink?

MARGARET: Tea?

LUCY: Tea? What am I? Eighty? Got a coffee?

MARGARET: I can get you some.

LUCY: Nah . . . I'm starving.

MARGARET: Starving?

LUCY: Not like Africa starving.

MARGARET: I was on a mission in Africa. Have you been?

LUCY: *(sarcastic)* Yeah, for Christmas.

MARGARET: Oh. I was in Nigeria for three years when I was, well, not much older than you.

LUCY: Did you help people?

MARGARET: No, no, our job was to make things worse.

LUCY: That's fucked.

MARGARET: Oh no, I'm making a joke.

LUCY: Weird joke.

MARGARET: I'm so sorry. I'm attempting irony.

LUCY: I don't know what you're saying.

MARGARET: We ran a girls' school. We financed a well. We brought antibiotics and—well, I don't want to toot our horn, but I like to think we helped.

LUCY: Didja give out condoms?

MARGARET: That wasn't our realm.

LUCY: I have low blood sugar. I could pass out any second.

MARGARET: Let's get some cookies in you then.

LUCY: You never had sex?

MARGARET: No. Have you?

LUCY: Yeah, I have a boyfriend. You're not even allowed to whack off?

MARGARET: Those are lovely tattoos. How many do you have?

LUCY: Four, well, three, and this one is half finished, on my back. This is a Sanskrit poem for peace, and that's my boyfriend's dick.

MARGARET: I see.

LUCY: Is Jesus your husband?

MARGARET: Is that what you wanted to ask me?

LUCY: Like a ghost? Like a succubus? Jesus Christ, Succubus?

MARGARET: Lucy, when you wrote, you said you wanted to ask . . . about your mother.

LUCY: But I don't really.

MARGARET: I'm sorry, I don't understand.

LUCY: I'm nervous.

MARGARET: Me too.

LUCY: I know.

MARGARET: Yes.

LUCY: I . . . *know*. About you. I know who you are.

MARGARET: I'm not sure what you / mean—

LUCY: I know what you did. I know who (*a burst of rage*) I AM! I KNOW WHO I AM! I know that if it wasn't for you, I wouldn't fucking be here, you BITCH!

Transition.

THE HOTEL ROOM

LIZ and MARYAM are in MARYAM's hotel room drinking the lovely wine.

LIZ: *L'Chaim.*

MARYAM: *(toast in Farsi) Beh salamati.*

They drink the lovely wine. It is nice. LIZ heads toward the mini bar.

Should we?

LIZ: Come on, it's a money-making event! It's run by the Jews.

MARYAM: Liz!

LIZ: What? I'm allowed to say it. We are being slightly Jewed down here, fee-wise—

MARYAM doesn't respond.

Please tell me you are being paid!

MARYAM: Yes, but I would do it for free.

LIZ: Oh no no no.

MARYAM: I am being paid a healthy honorarium.

LIZ: Uch. I don't want to hear "honorarium." How much?

MARYAM shakes her head.

Is it crude? To talk about? I'll tell you mine. Aren't you curious? You're curious. Come on. Tell me yours . . .

MARYAM beckons LIZ closer and whispers the number.

Eee. Well. G'night.

MARYAM: What?!

LIZ: It's for a good cause right?

MARYAM: You have to tell me now.

LIZ: No.

MARYAM motions for LIZ to tell. LIZ whispers.

MARYAM: No!

LIZ: Yes!

MARYAM: Well, but— /

LIZ: "Well, but."

MARYAM: —you've been doing these debates for years. This event tomorrow is all part of a book tour for me, and, and regardless, I'm giving mine to charity.

LIZ: Even more reason to pay you decently!

LIZ goes to MARYAM's mini-bar.

Catch.

She throws a bag of nuts at MARYAM.

Twenty-three dollars.

MARYAM catches it and LIZ *rifles through the fridge.*

M&M's, Snickers, V8, vodka—

They drink the vodka.

MARYAM: It really is too bad we're not on the same side.

LIZ: Not gonna ever happen.

MARYAM: Not just this debate. We're well-matched and it's too bad we don't play for the same side, isn't it?

LIZ: The expression is "playing for the same team."

MARYAM: *(shrugs, an explanation)* ESL.

LIZ: How would you say it in Farsi?

MARYAM: *Kash zire ye parcham boodim.* It means, "I wish we were under one flag." Fighting the same war.

LIZ: No thanks.

MARYAM: But it's a shame, because we have a lot in common.

LIZ: Ya think?

MARYAM: Of course we do! What are you afraid of?

LIZ: I'm not afraid . . .

MARYAM: Yes you are. In this moment, what are you afraid of?

LIZ: Not afraid . . . cautious.

MARYAM: Shall I tell you what I see, as I look at you?

LIZ: Okay . . .

MARYAM: You're afraid to know me. To feel something for me. As a person. But I'm not. I'm not afraid of what's between you and I.

   Pause.

LIZ: What is between you and I?

MARYAM: It's obvious we have a connection.

LIZ: Connection?

MARYAM: Yes . . . As friends.

   LIZ gets up.

LIZ: I should bounce.

MARYAM: You did not just say "bounce."

LIZ: (*as she finishes her lovely wine and gets up to leave*) I did. And I'm sticking with it.

MARYAM: You need to go?

LIZ: Don't I?

MARYAM: Do you?

LIZ: Do I?

MARYAM: Do you?

LIZ: Don't you think I do?

MARYAM: I want to show you something first.

LIZ: You don't really, though, do you?

MARYAM: I want to explain. Please.

MARYAM puts her hands on her heart.

This. My heart.

LIZ: Maryam, you have had almost nothing to eat, and a lot to drink—

MARYAM: Come closer.

LIZ: I'm actually fine over here.

MARYAM: No. Come here. Before I lose my nerve.

MARYAM pulls LIZ toward her and they sit.

MARYAM slowly removes her scarf. She beckons LIZ to come closer. MARYAM holds LIZ's hand and puts it on her chest and closes her eyes.

LIZ at first just sits there, then leans in, closer, closer, is about to kiss MARYAM's chest, when MARYAM suddenly opens her eyes and leaps up.

What are you doing?!

LIZ: Uh, misinterpreting—?!

MARYAM: I don't believe you!

LIZ: I'm sorry! / I—

MARYAM: Why would you do that?! Where would you get / the idea to—

LIZ: "My heart"?

MARYAM: Yes, *look* at my heart. My *scar*.

MARYAM points to her chest. There's a scar.

LIZ: Where?

MARYAM: Please don't pretend it's not obvious.

LIZ: Oh. That—

MARYAM: This is what I was trying to say we have in common.

LIZ: But—well—I don't—just say what you mean! Jesus!

MARYAM: I mean: I know what it's like. I've been between life and death; I know how people suffered, watching me suffer. I know about Stacey.

LIZ is stunned.

I understand why you would be so angry at god.

LIZ: Do you *"understand"* that Stacey died? Alone?

MARYAM: I didn't—

LIZ: Because she turned from a person *toward* god and there is no god? You understand?

MARYAM: You're missing / my point—

LIZ: No, I'm sorry you *"understand" me?* Because you went through something? A near-death experience? Which, by the way, is a chemical response that happens while you are still alive and can be scientifically measured, and you saw something? You saw / a light?

LIZ plows on. The two speeches below occur concurrently, overlapping—

MARYAM: I felt it. / I feel it! You don't know what I saw! What I went— Why would you ever say you know what someone feels or why! You don't know me. You dismiss what I experienced, what I'm trying to—

LIZ: You felt it, you feel it, you crossed the thin membrane between us and our spirits—you experienced something to give the world, and by the way, *you were flirting with me!!*

MARYAM: I was hoping to have a human connection, because I truly care about this debate!

LIZ: *You* obviously care about winning / this debate—!

MARYAM: I *believe* in something! It *matters*! You are old enough to be my mother. What are you? Fifty? The idea is disgusting.

LIZ: That is what all the closet-cased religious nutbars say before they're caught texting a teenager or fucking their nannies! That's what your religion does to people!

MARYAM: Or maybe I'm STRAIGHT!

LIZ: Yeah RIGHT!

MARYAM: Or maybe I changed my MIND.

> *LIZ slowly walks toward* MARYAM, *getting very close, intimate, then leaves, leaving* MARYAM *alone.* MARYAM *puts her scarf back around her neck. A soft light glows on* LIZ *in her seat at the debate, as she is watching* MARYAM *putting her scarf back on. We are in her memory for a moment.*

THE DEBATE

LIZ: Can we go back to something Maryam said earlier about the niqab?

RICHARD: I would like to pick up on this. Margaret, Yehudit, I know we haven't gotten to your remarks yet—

MARGARET: That's all right, Richard. I'm as patient as Job.

YEHUDIT: Job didn't have a choice, but go ahead.

RICHARD: Maryam, you were one of the lawyers on the team that supported the Canadian woman who didn't want to take off her niqab to testify in the trial of her accused rapist. It seems to me that an accused has a right to face his accuser, doesn't he?

MARYAM: And what about her rights? I thought we cared about her.

RICHARD: Would *you* wear a niqab?

MARYAM: No, Richard, I would not. Would you wear a leather jockstrap?

RICHARD: Where are we going with this?

MARYAM: Do you like my shoes? These cost three hundred dollars. That may or may not be more than the honorarium I am being paid to be here tonight. But these shoes help me express myself. I love them. The niqab is a form of self-expression. While I may not like low-rise jeans, I will fight for Liz's right to wear them.

LIZ: That's cute. You know what's not cute, but is actually appalling? You're fighting for a woman's right to be invisible. Richard could wear a leather jockstrap—

RICHARD: I may be wearing one right now—

LIZ: —and he will still be a white man who is controlling this debate.

RICHARD: *(to audience)* Controlling? I don't know about that . . .

LIZ: *(charming)* Don't you?

RICHARD: Not really.

LIZ: No? Richard's discreet cowhide underthings are not screaming to the world that he is someone's property. Erasable, unknowable.

In every society where women have been *seen*—empowered—the quality of life for the entire society improves. My opponent said that herself, at a speech at Carleton University / just last month—

MARYAM: What empowers women is the right to choose, no matter how unpleasant to the majority.

LIZ: Most women do not *choose* to wear the niqab!

MARYAM: But some do. I see *that* woman. I care about her, too. She may not be ready to remove it. She may not feel safe. It's the same as outing gay people—

LIZ: (*playing to audience*) Thaaat's a stretch!

MARYAM: Do you believe in outing gay people?

LIZ: Well. I want everyone to come out.

MARYAM: But would you force someone?

LIZ: Not in Uganda, but Canada, I hope I / wouldn't have to—

MARYAM: But / would you force them?

RICHARD: But *would* you?

MARGARET: You wouldn't.

YEHUDIT: Would you?

LIZ: It's not the same thing!

MARYAM: Honestly, in Quebec, Bill 62, the religious neutrality law: a bus driver can't even where a head scarf!

YEHUDIT: Or a kippa!

MARYAM: But a cross is okay.

YEHUDIT: Because that's Canadian.

MARYAM: There are maybe a dozen women wearing the niqab and one hundred politicians fighting it. Like taking a sledgehammer to kill a fly. What is it about really? Political point-scoring for the nationalist right wing in this country. It's so cynical I can barely dignify it by discussing it.

YEHUDIT: It's scapegoating. Oldest trick in the book.

MARYAM: The wild racists have been released by Trump—murdering worshippers in mosques and synagogues / putting children in cages—

LIZ: Look, Trump is Mussolini. BUT, the left has got to stop wussing out when it comes to women. We are afraid to say "don't wear a niqab" because we have to protect religious rights?!

YEHUDIT: In this climate, yes!

MARYAM: Now is not the time to be tacitly approving of Islamophobia—

LIZ: Instead, let's throw women under the bus. Let's *scapegoat* women.

RICHARD: Are you saying Liz is Islamophobic?

LIZ: No no no no no, let's be clear. It is not Islamophobic to criticize the niqab any more than it's anti-Semitic to say Lev Tahor is a cult or anti-Christian to say the church shelters pedophiles. That is why we're here, right, Margaret? Ayaan Hirsi Ali, who I've met, by the way—

RICHARD: Did you?

LIZ: Yes. She's more likeable in person. She's taller. She said, (reads) "It's not Islamophobic to point to those people who use the Quran to subject women and say, 'This is being done in the name of your religion, do something about it"—that's not Islamophobic, it's fair."

MARGARET: It's like when Jewish people say it's anti-Semitic to question Israel. And we all have questions about Israel!

YEHUDIT: Oy.

MARYAM: Would you agree with that, Liz? Am I anti-Semitic if I say Israel is an apartheid state?

YEHUDIT: EXCUSE me?

YEHUDIT shoots MARYAM a look. They look at each other. Beat.

LIZ: Apartheid is not a sound argument, if I were to make one, which I won't because I would prefer to be turned into a pillar of salt and drowned in a world-wide flood by a psychopathic god than talk about Israel and Palestine.

YEHUDIT: Exactly.

MARYAM: We can criticize Islam but we can't criticize Israel?

YEHUDIT: "Apartheid state" is not criticism, it's a false comparison; it's hurtful.

RICHARD: Let's stick with the niqab for now.

MARYAM: Our policy is clear. *(reads from her notes)* "Forcing a Muslim woman to remove her niqab has the potential to be a traumatic invasion of her privacy." In fact, it may discourage her from reporting sexual / assault.

LIZ: What discourages her is that she lives in a community where it's perfectly acceptable to "beat, whip, or scourge" / your wife for "disobedience," with a piece of wood—

YEHUDIT: There's no domestic violence in secular communities?! / Come ON!

MARYAM: That's / preposterous!

LIZ: —but I'm going to tell you honestly, and I would ask you all to be honest with yourselves. When you see a woman in a niqab, her face completely erased except for a slit for her eyes, her nose and mouth covered, her hands and her entire body draped in a heavy black tent, do you not have a visceral reaction? It *infuriates* me. It makes me feel like I am suffocating. I want her to take it off and let her skin feel the sun. To be free to run, to eat, to touch. I am furious with a system that dreamt up such a dismissing, oppressive, shaming practice that makes women invisible, and denies their own bodies. And while I agree that the state has no business forcing women to dress a certain way, in this case, I kind of hope they do.

MARYAM: You would have us believe that a Muslim woman cannot be trusted to know her own mind. How is that not racist?!

LIZ: Women can be misogynists; gay people can be homophobes!

MARYAM: Is that what you think I am? A naive Muslim woman trotted out to support the work of the evil fundamentalists?

LIZ: How else can I explain it?!

MARYAM: I just did!

RICHARD: Okay, let's not make this a debate exclusively about Islam because that *is* Islamophobic.

MARYAM: You were granted freedom by accident of birth. You have never had to struggle for it, and you don't appreciate its nuance and how hard you have to fight for it, even when you don't like it.

Lights shift and focus on MARYAM.

THE HOTEL ROOM

Lights up on a more drunk MARYAM *listening to loud music while pacing her hotel room, unnerved. "Miss World" by Hole. She rocks out, pushing herself, pushing through something— doubt, fear, attraction, trying to resist—suddenly she grabs her phone and texts. It appears on screen.*

"I want you to come here now."

We see the . . . symbol of LIZ *texting back.* MARYAM *paces, looking at her phone, waiting for a response. Then throws it down on the table.*

LIZ *enters.*

MARYAM *slowly walks toward* LIZ. LIZ *is not sure what the hell . . . she backs up.*

MARYAM *comes closer. They lean into each other. They start to kiss . . . Suddenly frenzied, urgent, they spin around, crashing into each other, desperate.* LIZ, *used to being in control, is surprised by* MARYAM *suddenly taking charge, and there is great, surprising tenderness between them for a beat.*

Lights.

THE DEBATE

Music plays as MARGARET'S *slide comes up over the podium. On the screen is a dated, non- professional picture and a bio that reads, "Margaret Donaghue, ex-nun, Catholic progressive advocate."*

MARGARET *has wandered close to the audience. She spots someone she knows in the crowd. She addresses the person.*

MARGARET: Oh, Sister Gene, it *is* you! I thought so! You've gotten so old. What memories. Nineteen sixty-seven, Vatican II, all of us young hippies joining together to spread the word of Christ. Oh look at your beautiful beads! Are those amber? Tiger eye? Sandstone? Oh well, what does it matter? Gene!

(to herself, a comment on how old Gene looks) My god.

As she walks back to the podium, she seems to get dizzy for a second. YEHUDIT *bolts over to steady her.* YEHUDIT *moves with speed, decisively and more powerfully than one might assume.*

Oh my, you're a real little cat.

YEHUDIT: That's my Israeli army training. In the days before you started calling it an apartheid state.

MARGARET: I never said apartheid.

RICHARD: *(calling from his spot)* That was Maryam. *(wanting to move things along)* You have two minutes, Margaret. *(chivalrous)* Well, you can have three.

MARGARET: Thank you, young man. It's taken me a minute just to get up here.

(to audience) As the director of the ethics committee at St. Mary's Catholic Hospital for twenty-seven years—

> *She responds to scattered applause from* RICHARD *and the audience.*

Thank you . . . I counselled pregnant teenagers who were so desperate for an abortion that they tried to poison themselves. I held their hands and walked them to our prenatal counsellors. And held their hands again when they delivered healthy babies into the arms of waiting, grateful Catholic families. I never, not once, *not one time* had doubt in my vocation.

Last fall, just over a year ago, a twenty-eight-year-old mother of four was rushed to our hospital, hemorrhaging from . . . everywhere. She was thirteen weeks pregnant. Both she and her baby were dying. The medical team informed us that one could be saved. And one could not. The baby, named Kathleen after her death, would die no matter what they did. The only one that could be saved was the mother.

So, save her, we said. She has four other children, a Catholic starter-family. She has a young husband pacing the hallways with his fists clenched against his chest. Save her, what's the problem? And they answered that the only way she could be saved was if her baby was aborted.

The medical team wanted to proceed with the abortion. Would I allow it?

At that moment, I felt as if I was teetering on a spike of ice at the top of god's highest precipice. All I could hear was wind and my pulse pounding in my throat.

I realized that my whole ethics team: Sister Judith, Pastor Raymond, Monica, Viv and the twins were holding their breath, waiting for my answer. It felt like forever, but it was probably forty seconds before I could speak . . . Yes, I would allow it. The doctors rushed out.

You all know what happened from there. Before I arrived home, I received notice from our bishop that because I allowed this abortion I was to be excommunicated.

It has been pointed out to me that priests accused of the sexual abuse of children take decades to be defrocked, if they ever are. More likely, like Cardinal Bernard Law, of Boston, they are transferred to Rome where they end up voting in the papal conclave. He resigned, himself, when he was eighty.

But for me, my life in the church was over in hours.

After a few days of a pyjamas and pasta pity party, I shook myself and thought: "No. I am not leaving my church. This is my church, and they can't have it!" I fought back, in my small way: I told my story. And I told it and I told it, and I told it, and I told it and my great-nephew Liam, bless him, put it on the YouTube, and the response in the last year has been . . .

Last week I received what Liam explained to me was a text—I thought it was an email, what on earth is the difference—a text from the young mother of four whose life was in our hands.

Apologizing for what she's put me through. A mother who lost her unborn child and nearly her life, apologizing to me: a childless forced-retiree who, for forty seconds, considered letting her die.

The world needs us, as Liam would say, to kick it old school. Back to Vatican II days. We need to reclaim Catholicism—emulating Jesus's love, compassion and mercy. Now, I know I've gone over my two minutes—

RICHARD: Have you?

MARGARET: Yes, well, I have one final point. My teammate and I may not agree on the existence of god—

LIZ responds from her seat.

LIZ: We were doing so *well*, Margaret . . .

MARGARET: Yes, but, we do agree that organized religion has a lot to answer for, and it won't, unless we, we women, who have been in the shadows, are brave enough to stand in the light, and ask the questions. Thank you.

RICHARD: Thank you.

He applauds, as do the other panellists.

MARGARET: All right, that's enough now. (*sternly*) That's *enough*.

Lights. The sound changes as MARGARET reacts and is isolated in a spot as her memory overtakes her again.

MARGARET'S OFFICE AT THE CATHOLIC HOSPITAL

Lights up on MARGARET's office. She and LUCY are back to their standoff. LUCY points to a file that MARGARET holds.

LUCY: "Sister Margaret Donaghue." And there *I* am. Fat baby girl.

MARGARET: How did you find me?

LUCY: There's this thing called the Internet. You can find anything and anyone. Police records, child welfare orders—you know the only place you can't get in? The church. Unless you got a dark-web guy who wants to finger you.

MARGARET: I can tell you, your mother loved you—

LUCY: You don't get to fucking tell me that my fucking mother loved me. My "mother" didn't even know she was pregnant. She was sixteen and retarded.

MARGARET: I don't like that word.

LUCY: *(mocking)* "I don't like that"—fuck you. She said to you, it says it right here, she didn't know what was happening to her!

MARGARET: That was a confession, Lucy. Said in a desperate time.

LUCY: Confess to what?? She didn't do anything.

MARGARET: You're in shock. It's a lot to take in— You need sugar—

LUCY: You know what I need? You to shut up, you full of shit old lady! My mom was mental, fucked, fucked in the head fucked. My dad raped her.

MARGARET: He didn't—

LUCY: . . . He *didn't*?!

She grabs the file, tossing pages on the floor, which MARGARET picks up.

Are you fucking crazy?! Vaginal abrasions. Internal bleeding. It's in your fucking file. Stop LYING! What is wrong with you people?! You can't stop!

MARGARET: But you were the good that came out of a—

LUCY: That's not what she thought! My mom didn't want to have that sick fuck's baby. No, she was like, I DON'T WANT THIS! But then some hospital asshole tells her these lies about what is going to happen to this hunk of cells with no brain yet, this jellyfish, this zombie baby, will wander through a void for eternity, and she will be tortured forever in hell if she doesn't have it! You used her like an incubator, like a puppy mill! To breed and then rip me away and give me to some "good Catholic family" who never even LOOKED for me when I left home, did you know that? Do you know what that feels like, Sister? Naw, and it's okay, it's okay, it's all okay now because now I know who I am. How do you like me so far?

MARGARET: Lucy—I, we believe in the sanctity of *life*—

LUCY: Sanctity?! I live in a squat. I sleep on a mattress that smells like dog piss that we dragged from a ravine. I shattered a homeless guy's kneecap with a hammer. *Why?* I get it *now*. I'm just like my dad. I got off on it. The way he screamed—

She screams, like the guy she tortured.

"Why would you do that?! Why?! What's the matter with you?!"

She hits her head to make it stop.

"Shut up!" "Shut up!" "Shut up!"

MARGARET: I'm sorry. Please. PLEASE stop. Shh shh Stop. Stop. Stop.

MARGARET tries to make LUCY stop hurting herself. LUCY breaks down. MARGARET holds her.

LUCY: Would you do it different now? If a girl came to you today . . . What would you do?

MARGARET pauses. She can't answer.

Answer me . . .

MARGARET: I don't . . .

LUCY: Answer!

MARGARET: I can't—I—

LUCY: WHAT WOULD YOU DO?! Would you help her? Would you!?

Beat.

MARGARET: I did.

Lights.

Transition.

RICHARD starts speaking downstage to the audience as LUCY exits, leaving MARGARET alone.

THE DEBATE

RICHARD: So, we have heard from three of our four panellists. Let's do a check-in. A straw poll. Are there audience members that think their opinions may have shifted based on what they have heard today? By applause. Ahh, interesting. Are there any of you who feel their opinions are more entrenched? By applause. Interesting. Okay. Some of you are just listening. Interesting. Well, that all may change again as we hear from our final panellist—Canada's first female Jewish Orthodox spiritual leader, author, educator, rabbah and mother of three. Thank for your patience, Yehudit Kalb.

YEHUDIT crosses to the podium. On the screen, a picture of YEHUDIT posed with her three kids appears, and her bio: "Modern Orthodox Jewish spiritual leader and author of Chas v'shalom, Change from Within, *Rabbah Yehudit Kalb."*

YEHUDIT: (*correcting pronunciation*) It's Yehudeeet.

RICHARD: (*trying again*) Yehuudit?

YEHUDIT: Close enough.

I'd like to begin with an old joke. A man is in the hospital, he's sick, and suddenly he hears the voice of God. God says, "I have good news and bad news. The good news is, there will be baseball in heaven. The bad news is you're pitching Thursday."

Polite laughter from the panellists. RICHARD *over-laughs.*

The Talmud asks, can you use as the side of your *suchah* an elephant? Do you know what a *suchah* is? It's like a ceremonial hut. We go into it in the fall, with a palm frond and an odd citrus fruit. Anyway, it's a harvest celebration, but in case you are wondering, the answer is yes, according to Talmudic debate, you can use an elephant as the side of a *suchah* because even if the elephant should die, God forbid, he or she still is going to be the requisite ten handspans for the *suchah* wall.

It used to be that discussing a woman as a *halachic* authority was like discussing an elephant as the wall of a *suchah*. It was purely theoretical. In Orthodox Judaism, women are no longer the elephant in the corner. We are the lioness in the centre!

Like Maryam, I have also experienced pushback from within. When I started studying at Yeshiva in Jerusalem, the men around me were even aggressively fighting my right to be there, but, very quickly, once they got to know me, they changed. They are now my greatest champions. If we *don't* abandon religion, it does progress.

On the other hand, let me remind you all of how secularism is doing in 2019 in terms of progress against misogyny: not that great. Oy. I wasn't even going to bring it up, but the ongoing trial of Harvey Weinstein, a secular, left-wing, feminist producer—

LIZ: #NotOurJew.

YEHUDIT: But we don't even have to go to that extreme. /

LIZ: Jeffrey Epstein, Brett Kavanaugh, / a church-going choirboy—

YEHUDIT: / We don't. Every day, young women go off to university and have a chance of being drugged and raped at a party, photographed naked and texted all over the world.

While those teenagers are vomiting out dorm windows, *our* teenage girls are studying Torah separately, safely, allowed to question and dream.

Because contrary to assumptions, the Torah does not ask women to be silent.

LIZ: Oh please—

YEHUDIT: Except maybe you. You could be a little silent.

> *LIZ appreciates that one.*

The Torah has very little to say about women, it's true, it was a reflection of its time. So we must closely look at the women who are given "air time." The mother of the Jewish people, Sarah, wife of Abraham, is said to have laughed when God told her she was pregnant at ninety. Laughed in the face of God's blessing? With joy? In shock? *At* God? Is this silence? In Orthodox Judaism, women are not servants in the home, but the *foundation* of the home.

LIZ: The basement—

YEHUDIT: We work, we lead, we are not submissive to any man—

LIZ: Just to god.

MARYAM: Richard, please!

RICHARD: Liz, you'll have a chance to rebut.

YEHUDIT: (*to* RICHARD) Could we bring up my slide again please?

RICHARD: (*into his headset mic*) Dominic?

> YEHUDIT *gestures to the screen, the slide of her with her children.*

YEHUDIT: These are my twin boys, Ephraim and Yizhak, and my daughter, Dinah. No offence to any other parents, but mine really are the cutest. I think it's interesting to note that neither of my opponents on the other side of this debate have children. One by virtue of religious belief, and one because of her choice of lifestyle.

LIZ: Wow.

> LIZ *writes notes after this one.*

YEHUDIT: My children let everyone know that women can be rabbahs, and no one can argue with them. I would like to close with a Hindu proverb: there are hundreds of paths up the mountain, all leading in the same direction. So it doesn't matter which path you choose. The only one who is wasting time is the one who runs around and around the mountain telling everyone that his or her path is wrong.

> *The lights change as* YEHUDIT *sits down.* LIZ *is champing at the bit to say something.*

LIZ: Richard, can I make a point?

RICHARD: If you have to—

LIZ: I do. Okay. Congratulations on your children who, despite growing up in a sheltered, backward cult manage to / impress.

MARYAM: Cult?!

YEHUDIT: This is why I didn't want to talk about my family!

LIZ: But ya did, Blanche! They are, indeed, the cutest. I saw some video at dinner last night.

RICHARD: You had a point?

LIZ: Yes, thank you. I wanted to address the comment that I don't have children because of my "choice of lifestyle." Small problem: it's not a choice, and it's not a lifestyle. I was "born that way." And although, thanks to *Orange is the New Black*, lesbianism may be stylish, it is not a life*style*, it's a life lived. And I really hope that lifestyle nonsense is not what you teach your kids.

YEHUDIT: We teach our children our own way. With stories—

LIZ: Bible stories?

YEHUDIT: Why not?

LIZ: Like Sodom and Gomorrah?

YEHUDIT: It's a great story. As any *parent* here knows, stories captivate children. They understand from them more than we know.

LIZ: Yes, they do!

RICHARD: *(to audience)* They agree! A miracle.

Liz, Bible stories? More dangerous than say, Grimms' fairy tales, or Cinderella for that matter?

LIZ: The Bible *is* a fairy tale that allows adults to kill *people*. Can we look at the little bit that's said in the Bible about women beyond Sarah's traumatic kick-in-the-guts hysteria triggered by the geriatric fertility tricks god was playing? Let's look at Sodom and Gomorrah. What's Lot's wife's name? Oh, that's right, "Lot's wife." And were Lot's daughters not offered up *first* to the people of Sodom and Gomorrah to rape, by their father, the most righteous man in Sodom, who would not allow his guests, god's angels, who Lot knew for five minutes, to be given to the Sodomites and Gomorreans for some vicious stranger sex? So instead he offered his *daughters*. My opponent alluded to rape culture at universities— where does she think it came from?! /

YEHUDIT: Again—

LIZ: According to the Talmud, if a woman is raped, she's supposed to marry her / rapist!

YEHUDIT: Again, these are interpretations. To be fair, the Talmud, in its time, was looking after the woman, the victim of the rape, who would have been devalued—

LIZ: Devalued?!

YEHUDIT: And perhaps abandoned by her community, as would her child, should there be one as a result of the / rape.

MARGARET: Terrible.

YEHUDIT: The Torah was protecting women and children. The Torah is realistic.

LIZ: That is the most preposterous, dangerous fucking thing I have heard in a long time.

The women react all at once.

YEHUDIT: Well.

MARGARET: Oh dear.

RICHARD: Our first F-bomb!

MARYAM: Is that really necessary?

LIZ: Yeah, I think it is.

YEHUDIT takes control.

YEHUDIT: No, no, this proves my point. Thank you, Liz. Many Jews have trauma and self-loathing to heal in themselves, and this is why this story is so important, so thank you. Listen closely, Liz, and see if it applies to you.

LIZ: It doesn't. / It's not real, it's a metaphor—

YEHUDIT: God commands Lot's wife—that's right, it's not real, it's a metaphor, right so, again, listen closely and see if you follow. Relax.

LIZ: Ooh boy.

YEHUDIT: It's a story. God commands Lot's wife to not look back as her family flees for their lives from the apocalyptic disaster, the burning cities of Sodom and Gomorrah, but she can't resist.

God knew that women look back, women are the keepers of memory. And for looking back, in nostalgia, in regret, in heartfelt empathy with the squealing animals running around with their fur on fire, Lot's wife, this ordinary nameless mother, is turned into a pillar of salt! What an arresting image—salt tears, bitterness, loss. This story is extraordinary, isn't it? That's why I love it—

LIZ: You love it.

YEHUDIT: It's fantastic! These stories, *our* stories, are fully relevant to our modern struggles—and that's why we all know them. Even you.

LIZ: I know "Jack and the Beanstalk" too, but I wouldn't try and live my life by it.

YEHUDIT: In these debates we are deliberately suspending our intelligence! These stories are our subconscious made literate. You don't deny there are aspects of our lives that cannot be explained by scientific fact?

LIZ: Yet.

YEHUDIT: Liz, we are not just bags of flesh, kalumphing on the planet for seventy-five years for no reason! Look at your own teammate. Look what she's accomplished in her life., She didn't have children of her own, but imagine the people she's helped and still helps. For her god.

MARGARET: Well . . . I—

YEHUDIT: My mother was a difficult woman. We clashed, I admit. But she was filled with *shechinah*, God's female presence. When she was dying, she looked at me, only me, right before she went, and I saw the Sadieness of her vanish. The energy in the room faded, like a dimmer switch drawn down. What was left on that hospital bed was body, but who she *was*, was *neshamah*, soul.

RICHARD: What do you think about soul, Liz?

LIZ: I want to kill myself when Bruno Mars comes on the radio.

Beat. She smiles at the audience. Then gets serious again.

Look, we are afraid of death. So, we create a beautiful way out. Fifty percent of Americans believe they will see their pets in heaven. I prefer to face the fear and not indulge in fantasy of some magical hereafter with seventy-two virgins and rivers of wine and milk. Dead is dead.

MARYAM: So your late partner, you don't think you will see her again?

Beat.

LIZ: I do not.

MARYAM: She is gone and whatever was unresolved will never be resolved?

LIZ: Yes.

MARYAM: Whatever is unforgiven will remain so.

LIZ: Yes.

YEHUDIT: *Chas ve Shalom. [God forbid.]*

MARYAM: *Khoda nakoneh. [God forbid.]*

MARGARET: Heaven forfend.

MARYAM: *Zabanam lal. [May my tongue be silenced.]*

LIZ: Jesus Christ!

LIZ looks to MARYAM.

Lights. Loud music. YEHUDIT bolts up, goes to her mother, her emah, SADIE, and collapses in her arms.

YEHUDIT'S SISTER'S WEDDING

YEHUDIT: Emah, Emah . . .

SADIE tries to comfort her daughter but is actually a bit irritated.

SADIE: Stop. Stop. Snap out of it. There we go. Yehudit. That's it. Let it out. But keep it together.

Eventually YEHUDIT calms down.

Yofi. Yehudit, *sheynaleh,* let him go. Trust me. You'll be happier.

YEHUDIT: Are you happy?

SADIE: If I was any happier I would spit. Now pull yourself together and go apologize to your sister.

YEHUDIT: I'm not sorry! I love Ezra!

SADIE: Uch! *(like she's spitting)* "Love"!

YEHUDIT: He loves me, too.

SADIE: It doesn't matter! "Love." *Bubbaleh*, sh. Listen to me, you have *sechel [brains]*. Your sister, what does she have? Beauty fades. Now, I want you to get out there and sit with your sister and put a smile on your face.

YEHUDIT: No! I'm going to the men's side to find Ezra.

SADIE: You will NOT.

SADIE grabs her arm.

YEHUDIT: He loves me. He, I—we—

SADIE: I don't want to hear. / Don't say it!

YEHUDIT: You don't know what this feels like.

SADIE: It's a feeling! It will pass.

YEHUDIT: No, this feeling will never pass because I'll never let it go.

SADIE: Life is long. Love is a *rash*. It burns and it itches and then it passes and you forget all about it. And if you're lucky you still are left with your own skin underneath it all—

YEHUDIT: No.

SADIE: Yes, because, *Maidaleh*, that's all you've got. Yourself. That's it. *Shoin*. Now be brave.

YEHUDIT: No. No. I'm not going to be like you. Married to someone I hate and stuck with kids I resent. I do have *sechel*, Emah, but I'm not *all sechel*! And I am going to have love. I'm going to have a life that *means* something, that changes everything, so no girl has to grow up and become like YOU.

SADIE slaps her across the face. YEHUDIT is shocked.

SADIE: This is why I chose Ezra for your sister and not for you.

YEHUDIT: *YOU* chose him?

SADIE: Today is your sister's day. Yours will come, *Hashem* help us when it does.

SADIE tries to take YEHUDIT back to the wedding.

Suddenly, YEHUDIT runs into the men's side of the wedding.

YEHUDIT: Ezra!

Ugly, vicious, sustained yells of male protest erupt from the men's side. She is thrown out. She collapses on the floor breathing heavily.

The lights change.

MARYAM and LIZ walk slowly downstage in shafts of light facing the audience. They are also breathing heavily. Their breath turns into the sound of approaching orgasms as they each step up on the beam in shafts of light and face the audience. After her orgasm, LIZ's sound turns into sobbing. MARYAM comes to her and touches her and LIZ collapses into MARYAM's arms. Holding each other tightly, LIZ gathers herself.

Now we are in:

THE HOTEL ROOM

From their embrace:

LIZ: Oh god.

MARYAM: Oh no.

LIZ: Oh Jesus.

MARYAM: You know, for an atheist you mention god a lot.

LIZ: God metaphorically. I'm reclaiming the word god to describe the ecstatic feeling that we all as human beings feel—

MARYAM puts her hands on LIZ's face.

MARYAM: Shhh.

MARYAM's touch moves LIZ.

I don't understand . . . It's been a long time?

LIZ: Sorry sorry—

MARYAM: It's the *first* time since . . . ?

LIZ: Not that there haven't been offers.

MARYAM: Have there been?

LIZ: No.

MARYAM laughs. Beat between them.

This is—

MARYAM: This is not— / I mean—

LIZ: Right? I should just—

MARYAM: Okay.

LIZ: Okay.

MARYAM: Okay?

LIZ: Okay.

    Beat.

I'll just get a drink and I'll—

MARYAM: Don't say bounce.

    They laugh.

LIZ: I just have one . . . ?

MARYAM: Yes?

LIZ: You've done this before . . . ?

MARYAM: Can I say something?

LIZ: Yes.

MARYAM: It's almost like you haven't.

LIZ: Ahh.

MARYAM: There was one / in college.

LIZ: Please don't say college. AHH! We should just say good night and pretend this / never happened.

MARYAM: Good night—

They touch and it stops them both in their tracks.

LIZ: Jesus—

MARYAM: STOP.

LIZ: Goddamn it . . . Christ!

LIZ gets a drink.

Do you really have a heart condition?

MARYAM: Yes! What? Do you think I show my scar to—

LIZ: I don't know—

MARYAM: It's my opening line—?

LIZ: Well, it's a really good one. So?

MARYAM: Well, yes and no. It's still very fresh.

LIZ: Uh-huh . . .

Beat.

So are you . . . ?

MARYAM: I don't believe in labels.

LIZ: *(quoting MARYAM's labels)* Iranian, Canadian, Moderate Muslim—

MARYAM: *(correcting) Progressive* Muslim—

LIZ: Lawyer. And . . . ?

MARYAM: Fluid.

LIZ: Ich! That's just the new "bi." It means undecided.

MARYAM: That makes you sound old.

LIZ: I am.

MARYAM: Do you know what my mother did in Tehran?

LIZ: I do. And that was a really nice time to bring up your mother.

MARYAM: Well?

LIZ: She was a translator.

MARYAM: You googled my family!

LIZ: Know your enemy.

MARYAM: Did you know she was a professor of engineering? Before the revolution?

LIZ: Impressive.

MARYAM: Is it? Why?

LIZ: No, I don't—

MARYAM: It's amazing what those backward people can learn.

LIZ: No, it's impressive to me because I have no spatial or mathematical sense. But, fair enough.

MARYAM: Fair enough? If only we could say that tomorrow, there would be no debate.

LIZ: And that would be a shame.

MARYAM: Would it?

LIZ: Yes. As I already said, cha-ching—

    Beat.

So. Your mother.

MARYAM: Well, so, of course, she was a force. She wanted better for me, my sisters, my brother.

LIZ: You have a brother?

MARYAM: You didn't know?

LIZ: You don't mention him on the interweb!

MARYAM: Ah ha! Well, I have a brother.

LIZ: Do you want to . . . talk . . . about him?

MARYAM: No, thank you.

LIZ: I have a brother who I don't speak to. He's a bit of an ass.

MARYAM: Can I tell you about my brother?

LIZ: You just said—

MARYAM: I was being polite. It's called *Tarof*. I was *Tarofing*. We say no to the first offer, but you need to ask me a second time. We do it with cookies, and so, with family stories.

LIZ: Tell me about . . .

MARYAM: Faraz.

LIZ: Faraz. Tell me.

> *Pause. There is much sweetness and intimacy between them.*
> MARYAM *is unsure.*

MARYAM: Tell me about Stacey.

LIZ: You already know everything apparently.

MARYAM: Tell me something I don't know.

> LIZ *gets another drink.*

LIZ: After the diagnosis—

MARYAM: Before the diagnosis.

> *Under this* LIZ *offers* MARYAM *wine, which* MARYAM *declines, so she offers her a second time—Tarofing.*

LIZ: Before the diagnosis, that's not so interesting.

MARYAM: You still loved each other after ten years? No kids?

LIZ: Love changes.

MARYAM: I have no idea what that means.

LIZ: . . . I took her for granted.

MARYAM: You had an affair?

LIZ: What's that look?

MARYAM: I don't lie.

LIZ: But you do *this*?

MARYAM: We were talking about your / affair.

LIZ: It wasn't . . . Life is not that simple, my dear. Maybe in your world.

MARYAM: My world is one in which I am not patronized.

Beat.

LIZ: Sorry.

MARYAM: Stacey found out about the affair, and it was . . . ?

LIZ: Biblical. She rent her garments, threw things—her shoes, her running shoes from 1995 that she refused to . . .

MARYAM: And you?

Beat.

LIZ: I shoved her.

MARYAM: Oh.

LIZ: I was trying to contain her. She could have—

MARYAM: Could she?

Beat.

And then . . . ?

LIZ: I was sleeping at my friend Maggie's when I got the text.

MARYAM: She told you her diagnosis by text?

LIZ: She did. And I came back. One hundred percent. I came back.

Beat. LIZ leans in closer to MARYAM.

So. Faraz.

MARYAM: No . . . You . . .

MARYAM kisses LIZ sensually.

Transition.

MARGARET'S OFFICE AT THE CATHOLIC HOSPITAL

It is not long after LUCY's visit. MARGARET picks up LUCY's file. She searches through it, pulls out some pages, rips them up.

Her office phone rings. She doesn't answer it. She crumples the paper as she backs away from the phone, waiting for it to stop ringing.

MARGARET: Leave me alone . . . Leave me alone . . . Leave me alone.

Lights.

THE DEBATE

RICHARD, YEHUDIT, MARGARET and LIZ are laughing as we transition back. The panellists are giddy.

YEHUDIT: Okay, okay, so, a very orthodox man, Sauly, is praying every day. He just wants to win the lottery. Every day he prays and prays and he never wins. Finally, he calls out to the Lord, "Hashem, I pray every day to you to win the lottery, but I never win! What am I doing wrong?" And all of a sudden there's this booming voice comes out of the heavens, "Sauly . . . buy a ticket."

They laugh.

LIZ: Okay, okay, so—a ship is sinking and the captain asks, "Does anyone here know how to pray?" And one person speaks up, I do, I do, and the captain says, "Good, you stay here and pray, we're one life jacket short." .

YEHUDIT: Okay, okay, I got another one. A little boy comes home from Hebrew school and he tells his mother, "Emah, Emah, I got a part in the play!" "What's the part?" "The part of the Jewish Husband." And the mother says, "You march right back there and tell them to give you a speaking part!"

RICHARD, YEHUDIT, LIZ and MARGARET laugh. MARYAM is not amused.

MARGARET: What do you call a nun on an electric scooter . . . ? Virgin Mobile.

They all laugh, except MARYAM.

LIZ: Don't be jealous, Maryam. I'm sure we could find some Muslim jokes too.

MARYAM: I'm sure I don't want to hear them.

RICHARD: Okay, okay, we're all getting giddy, but let's just be serious for a second.

Beat.

A Jew, a Muslim and a Christian walk into a bar and the bartender says, "Is this some kind of joke!?"

They all laugh, but he laughs longest.

All right, Liz, I noticed your joke was about prayer—

LIZ: Hilarious.

RICHARD: —and I've always wondered this, seriously, as an atheist, haven't there been times in your life when you envy people who receive comfort from faith?

LIZ: You just outed yourself.

RICHARD: That will be news to my wife.

LIZ: Well, you're United Church, right?

RICHARD: Um, yes, but what is United anyway?

LIZ: "Jesus is your GPS"? Title of your speech to the Toronto United Church conference in 2015?

RICHARD: This is not about me.

LIZ: Isn't it?

RICHARD: Listen carefully, I'm asking about you.

LIZ: I am listening, sir.

RICHARD: I'm not your enemy here.

LIZ: Could you mansplain that to me?

MARYAM: He's doing his best.

YEHUDIT: There are rules.

MARGARET: It's a tough position to be in.

LIZ: Well, then it's good that he's got all three of you to protect him.

Beat. No one is on LIZ'*s side on this one.*

Yes, there are times I envy that comfort. I used to pray, at Yom Kippur in the balcony with the other inconsequential women, for no more Holocausts, Halloween treats and a dog. I got the dog. I bet many adults would love to have that childish feeling of comfort, Richard, when the chips are down, but they *know* that life is real and short and best lived that way.

MARYAM: *Your* way.

LIZ: If women could feel what they really feel, Maryam, and say what they mean, it would be a game-changer.

RICHARD: Margaret, do you agree with Liz about prayer? That it's simply a childish panacea.

MARGARET: Well, no, I mean, I do agree that prayer is not cause and effect, and I have compassion for Liz, and for anyone who loses a spouse of any sort, of gender or—type of—sex—

RICHARD: (*rescuing her*) Sure, sure—

MARGARET: But the truth is, Liz, I know and I, I *insist*, that prayer allows me to feel *more* deeply what I really feel, not less.

LIZ: And it's just a matter of time before you let that go too.

MARYAM: It sounds like you want to control what a woman believes the same way you say religion wants to control women!

LIZ: I don't want to control you. I want you to stop allowing yourself to be brainwashed!

MARYAM: So you can brainwash me?

LIZ: I'm sorry, in your case, that would be impossible.

MARYAM: Because I am more than just flesh and ambition. I am part of a oneness that's bigger than us as individuals, and I am sad for you that you will always be angry and alone.

Beat. Everyone is taken aback by that personal jab.

LIZ: Comfort and joy.

RICHARD: Maryam, my question / was—

MARYAM: Your question was important. Prayer does provide comfort. And healing. Miraculous healing. Doctors now have proof that prayer can affect / medical outcomes—

LIZ: That's junk science.

MARYAM: No, it's / medically proven—

YEHUDIT: Even if it is not true, though, do you hold all of science responsible for the junk notions?

LIZ: Science doesn't ask us to *worship* it's / junk notions.

YEHUDIT: Wait, think about this analogy. Use your *sechel* for a moment. Do you believe the junk notion that says your thoughts can control whether you beat cancer or not? Do you believe that?

LIZ: No, of course not.

YEHUDIT: But—

MARYAM writes a note to YEHUDIT. YEHUDIT reads:

But your partner did, yes?

> *Beat. LIZ looks at MARYAM, betrayed, shocked—what did she tell YEHUDIT?*

LIZ: I—I thought we weren't talking about our families.

RICHARD: You said you were an open book, Liz.

MARGARET: Come on now, Richard.

YEHUDIT: Maybe it was you that she needed the most. But you are not bigger than cancer. She needed more. We all do. So, you can't control *shysters* from using junk science to sell *The Secret* DVDs, and you can't control ignorant people from hijacking religion to harm women.

LIZ: Ignorant people? Are you ignorant?

YEHUDIT: Excuse me?

RICHARD: What?

MARYAM: What?!

LIZ: I can quote Yehudit from a rabbinical conference last fall where she said that a woman should submit to her husband in her household. How many *equals* submit?

YEHUDIT: That's not what I meant—

MARYAM: It's not / what she meant.

LIZ: A woman as smart as you, acting submissive so they'll let you in the club? What did you have to sacrifice to get in, Rabbah? And they never did let you in, did they?

YEHUDIT: *I* have not sacrificed anything. I have children and a husband—

LIZ: Why did you not get married until you were thirty? Most people in your community have three kids by twenty-three.

MARYAM: Now you care about / marriage?!

LIZ: Denied love and touch until you were thirty! Your religions try to control women's sexual power / and they are losing!

YEHUDIT: We don't try to control it—we just don't let it run amok!

LIZ: I understand your husband is not allowed to look at your vagina during sex. Will he burst into flames?

MARGARET: Sex sex sex—

LIZ: What did you mean when you said that Orthodox Judaism can *never* accept homosexuality?

MARYAM: We've covered this.

LIZ: (*reading*) "Gay relationships are unnatural, an abomination, a disease, / anti-Jewish."

YEHUDIT interrupts but LIZ steamrolls.

YEHUDIT: We don't mean "abominations" in the / Christian sense.

LIZ: I am *quoting you* from a lovely Orthodox seminar that the audience can find on YouTube! What did you mean?!

MARYAM: What do *you* mean?

LIZ: Actually, I take it back.

LIZ gets up suddenly and approaches YEHUDIT right at her table.

You're not ignorant.

She turns around.

I turn all the way around. *Teshuvah.* Forgive me? She's not ignorant. She's deluded.

All start talking at once, on their feet.

MARYAM: *You're* deluded!

YEHUDIT: It's okay, / Maryam, it's okay—

MARYAM: It's not okay! / It's not!

LIZ: Am I / forgiven? Am I?!

YEHUDIT: Maryam, don't / bite—

MARGARET: Stop. Stop. Will you stop, she apologized! She apologized!! Just STOP!

MARGARET stands up. Lights isolate her.

MARGARET moves into her memory. She sits on the beam.

MARGARET ALONE

MARGARET: . . . Maybe she slipped . . .

Mary, hear me . . . Jesus, comfort me . . . she could have slipped . . . the four boys, those four little boys going everywhere together singing. Arms around each other. One started and the other would jump in, and then all four, their voices leaping over each other like puppies. And they'd go to get water from the well that we were building and Sister Mercy and I would ever so quietly try to join in.

She sings.

On the way to the well there was that long wooden bridge, a plank, over the dried-out riverbed way down below.

The boys would stand teetering on this narrow plank. We could barely look, it would be so easy to slip off and disappear . . . They'd balance and then scamper across screaming, laughing on the other side. One night, Sister Mercy and I decided to try it. There was a full, silver moon. It was so bright. I put my foot on the thin plank of wood, and up I stood. Oh.

It was like being dunked into freezing cold water. My heart was pounding, my stomach clenched. I felt so alive. How easy it would be to let go, and to leap. If we could, we would all leap, wouldn't we, into the air, and let god catch us? And I did it. I leapt. I leapt back to the ground. I couldn't run across like those boys, could I?

Jesus, forgive me . . . She was drunk, probably . . . yes . . .

Under this, a barely lit LUCY *stands as if she's teetering on an edge in* MARGARET's *memory.*

Foot up on the viaduct, the grab of fear, the dark dry river of the DVP below, a blinding light of an oncoming truck, a horn . . . she could have slipped, couldn't she . . . ? But why *wouldn't* you leap? If no one listened, if no one answered your call, no one could summon up the least bit of courage to say I'm sorry! Jesus, Mary . . . I hope she regretted. I really do, in her last panicked, terrified moments, I hope she flailed in the air and tried to turn around. I hope she was filled with *shame* . . . I just wanted her to go away . . . that's the truth. I just wanted her to go away and never to come back. I wanted to forget her . . . Please wash this away. Help me. Please forgive me . . . I can feel your love, I can . . . Please, just. Stop.

THE HOTEL ROOM

Music. Later. Post-sex again.

LIZ: Tell me. Tell me. Tell me. Tell me.

MARYAM: Ask me. What you like.

LIZ: What does he look like?

MARYAM: Tall. His legs are to your waist. He's much older than me. Almost your age.

LIZ: Wow. He's the crypt keeper.

MARYAM: He loves to walk. That's his "thing." I can't keep up with him. The only one who could was my auntie.

LIZ: Is she in Toronto?

MARYAM: No, she's still in Tehran, the youngest of my mother's sisters, and she got all the legs. She was a botanist. She would splice plants and make new ones, you know?

LIZ: Riveting.

MARYAM: Yes, and I was told my brother found it peaceful because his mind was always whirring, you know, with this idea, and that outrage about the regime. He was—like you!

LIZ: Thank you.

MARYAM: He was troubled.

LIZ: Hey!

　　Beat.

And?

MARYAM: And one day my auntie and Faraz were walking and it got quite late.

LIZ: How old were you?

MARYAM: No, I wasn't born yet. He was fifteen. She was maybe twenty-five.

LIZ: And they were walking?

MARYAM: On our street, and it was dark. You know, at that time, it was not long after the revolution and a woman could not be walking with a man who was not her relative, but they were relatives so—and they were laughing—

LIZ: Oh no.

MARYAM: So, a gang of men, all in black—

LIZ: Revolutionary Guard?

MARYAM: Might not have been. We never found out. They surround them, "It's funny to be with a woman who's not your wife?!" My auntie was beaten, her clothes were—she—my brother, his face was so swollen, my mother screamed and screamed in the hospital when she saw him. They had to give her sedation. The only thing my auntie says to me about it is, "It was like they were playing cricket with his head." And while it was happening, and this is on our street, you understand, and our neighbours were crying, "She's his auntie! She's his auntie!" which made them more— Our neighbours dragged Faraz to a pickup truck, to the hospital. They should probably never have moved him.

LIZ: And now?

MARYAM: And now he is suspended in time. He doesn't remember anything after the attack. He doesn't know we are in Canada. He doesn't . . . know me. He thinks I'm my auntie. I don't exist for him because I was born after the attack, which he thinks was yesterday.

LIZ: Does he remember being attacked?

MARYAM: He remembers being *rescued*. He says it was a *Mojezeh*, a miracle. "Look at me! Not a scratch! A miracle from Allah! *Mojezeh*! I'm healed! Life is good!" He doesn't remember the eight years of physio. Every day he wakes up and experiences salvation. And so my anti-religious brother has become devout.

LIZ: So how can you . . .

MARYAM: Yes . . . ?

LIZ: I don't understand why you still believe in god, much less Islam.

MARYAM: Because we can't let them win. We can't abandon Islam to hoodlums like them. They saw everything in black and white, them and us. I can never support a view like yours that accepts no shade of grey—

LIZ: Okay.

MARYAM: What?

LIZ: I respect what you're saying.

MARYAM: And?

LIZ: That's it.

MARYAM: Say what you think!

LIZ: Look, I'm glad you told me, and I think it's sad.

MARYAM: You're lying to me.

LIZ: No, I'm not. It's sad.

MARYAM: That's all?

LIZ: That's all.

MARYAM: It's not going to affect whether I see you again, or maybe it will, if you don't tell me the truth!

LIZ: It's outrageous! It shouldn't have happened.

MARYAM: But had it not happened, I would never have been born. I was my parents' grief baby. And we would never have come here, and I would not be a lawyer able to defend the rights of my sisters. That's the miracle!

LIZ: That . . . is . . . some twisted logic.

MARYAM: Life is like that, actually. For most of the world.

LIZ: I know, but—I don't see it that way.

MARYAM: You don't see my life that way?

LIZ: No.

> *Beat.*

MARYAM: You can't say anything to anyone and this can't happen again.

> *LIZ is shocked. Lights.*

LIZ: No! No no—wait—no—

THE DEBATE

> *LIZ and MARYAM seamlessly are back at their chairs.*

LIZ: NO NO NO. Wait wait. What / did you just say?!

MARYAM: I *have* said that Islam, like *all* religions, has to be held to account for how it treats women, but the negative / is *all* you—

LIZ: Islam is *not* like all religions.

MARYAM: (*to the others*) Did you hear that?! / Now it's coming out!

LIZ: It is NOT. It's time for some real *honesty* from you people / for a change.

MARYAM: "You people"?! You people?! Who is being honest here and who is hiding behind dogma?! You or us!

LIZ: What Margaret did, abandoning her church, her community, her sisters who she lived with and ate with and sang with and cried with for forty years, that's *courage*.

MARGARET: Not courage, not courage—

LIZ: *That's* a movement. Can you imagine how alone she feels in her little bachelor apartment in this fucking city where we throw old women away?! Even Yehudit is taking on the orthodox patriarchy— /

YEHUDIT: Wow—

MARYAM: You don't believe that for one / second!

RICHARD: To be fair, / you don't, Liz.

LIZ: (*to RICHARD*) You? Fair? I could have swept this thing if you hadn't saddled me with Sister Sunshine over here.

MARGARET: You listen here, I am filled with the love of Christ. Filled with it! Jesus loves me and that's how I can love you / despite the fact that you are a destructive—

LIZ: No, no no, THANK you! Keep your Jesus love to yourself! The cruellest things that were said to us, when Stacey was dying, were said by Christians—

MARGARET: Yes, yes, let it GO! Life is not fair. People we love die and we *move on*. That's what Mary did. That's what women DO!

Beat.

LIZ: Would you ever have left the church if they hadn't kicked you out . . . ? Would you?

MARGARET hesitates.

MARGARET: No . . . I wouldn't have. God forgive me. I wouldn't have done anything.

MARYAM: That's / enough, Liz.

YEHUDIT: She's doing something / *now.*

RICHARD: Let's all calm down—

LIZ: But you really are the worst, Maryam. You are happy to be just sitting there right in the middle, trying to have your cake and eat it too when they don't actually—

YEHUDIT: She's the bravest / of all of us!

LIZ: —they don't want you. They don't—if they knew who you were, if they knew what you did last night, / they wouldn't want you.

RICHARD: Last night? At the dinner?

MARYAM: The teams in this debate are actually all three of us, *trying*, against you, *ripping things apart*! You are blinded by rage.

LIZ: And why the hell shouldn't I be?! What's wrong with all of you / that you're not?!

MARYAM gets up and crosses downstage to address the audience.

MARYAM: If you think *this* is the future, this is the better way, then vote for them, but if you think there is *any* chance that we could all believe what we want, in peace, then you *must* vote for us. Vote for freedom of choice—

LIZ: Freedom from hypocrisy!

MARYAM: Intolerance!

LIZ: SECRETS!

MARYAM comes back toward LIZ.

MARYAM: Don't!

LIZ: Why not? What's going to happen? What will they / do to you?

MARYAM: You promised! You promised!

RICHARD: Promised what?

MARYAM: Nothing!

RICHARD: Did you two promise each other something / before this debate?!

LIZ: No, no, let's just—

MARYAM: Liz—

LIZ: —pretend—

MARYAM: Please—

LIZ: —that you did not text me last night and ask me to come to your room.

MARYAM: Oh god.

LIZ: That you did not crack me open and then just expect me to walk away. Is this what you do?

YEHUDIT: What? NO! Oh no. Oh no NO!

YEHUDIT leaps up and looks at MARYAM and LIZ—are her suspicions right? Yes. LIZ holds her head in her hands. Starts to breathe hard. She can't believe what she's just done.

MARYAM: Yehudit, it's not—

YEHUDIT: Do you think I'm stupid?! / I'm not stupid! I am not stupid!

RICHARD boots downstage and talks charmingly to the audience.

RICHARD: Ladies and gentlemen, I think we will just go ahead and leap into the voting. So, should women abandon religion? If you have been convinced—

(into his headset) / Yes, Dominic? You're not ready?!

He listens.

YEHUDIT: Did you two have sex with each other last night?

MARYAM: No, we didn't. It wasn't like that. Liz, tell her the truth.

LIZ can't answer. YEHUDIT sees that. She goes to MARGARET.

YEHUDIT: (*to MARGARET*) Do you see what's happening here?

MARGARET: No.

MARYAM: It's not— / Liz, tell her, tell her!

YEHUDIT: It's not WHAT?

(*to LIZ*) And YOU! You just put a suicide vest on your career and HERS and blew it up!!

MARYAM's breathing is shallow.

MARYAM: Listen, look, it's not, oh—

MARYAM tries to catch her breath. She slumps forward. LIZ and YEHUDIT bolt to her.

LIZ: Are you okay?

YEHUDIT: What's wrong with her?

LIZ: She has a heart thing.

LIZ lays MARYAM down and stays with her.

MARGARET: Juice! Get her juice. I worked in a Catholic hospital for twenty-seven years—juice!

MARYAM's trying to regain her emotions.

MARYAM: I'm fine. I faint sometimes. I'm okay, please. It's embarrassing.

RICHARD: You're fine?

MARYAM: Yes. Yes.

RICHARD: *(to Dominic)* Music!

(to audience) Okay, folks, no one panic, she's fine, she faints sometimes, but we do need to record an ending to the debate, so talk amongst yourselves, listen to the music and stick around for the vote!

Pithy music pipes into the theatre.

(talking in his headset to Dominic) We have to edit all that shit out—no, it isn't good fucking TV—it makes the whole thing look like a fucking fuck-fest joke! Yeah, we all have kids we don't see, Dominic!

YEHUDIT: *(to LIZ, a realization)* . . . You set this up.

LIZ: What? No, I didn't—

MARYAM: It was my *choice.*

YEHUDIT: No no, I see I see, I see. It wasn't just reckless and thoughtless fumbling like animals / like—

RICHARD: (*to Dominic*) Fer the love of Jesus COCK am I the only CUNTING professional on this motherfucking stage?! CHECK THE PLAYBACK!! you dumb-ass!

MARGARET: Oh my goodness!

YEHUDIT: She *used* you!

MARYAM: I do not get USED.

YEHUDIT: Margaret!

MARGARET: I'm sorry, my dear, I'm not—

YEHUDIT: She's been saying all along, "You can't have your cake and eat it too," and now she's using you to prove her point!

MARYAM: She's not *using* me to do anything. You don't know / me!

YEHUDIT: If that's not what she's doing then what *you* did was, what? Just for lust? / For fun—

MARYAM: For life, for connection, for—

YEHUDIT: For what?

    YEHUDIT looks at LIZ *and* MARYAM, *who share a vulnerable loaded look.*

For *love*?! HA! HA!

    YEHUDIT points at LIZ *and laughs.*

MARYAM: What / happened to you?

YEHUDIT: Love?! Do you hear this nonsense?! Love is a RASH! It consumes and disfigures you and then one day it's gone and all you are left with is rough skin and homeopathic creams, and you are alone! Love? *Shoin.* Then this is even more despicable! Undignified!! Unworthy! / Unholy!

MARYAM: What happened to you?! What is wrong with you?! / What is wrong with you?!

YEHUDIT: It's not fair! It's not right! It's not right! You're not right! You are not right! You're doing the wrong thing!

MARGARET: Oh, my dears.

    RICHARD storms over

RICHARD: Oh my dears nothing! You are all going to SIT back down and pretend that you care about your *ideas*! Unique! Ideas! Now! You are going to do this for the cameras! And you (*MARYAM*) are going to do something for someone who you *aren't* fucking!

YEHUDIT: I'm going HOME.

RICHARD: No you're not.

    RICHARD blocks YEHUDIT's path. YEHUDIT won't be blocked.
    RICHARD grabs her wrist as she passes him.

    YEHUDIT does a quick, vicious Krav Maga move on RICHARD.
    Twisting his wrist, shoulder and then breaking his nose.
    MARYAM, LIZ and MARGARET are shocked and jump in to try
    and stop this sudden violence. They pivot like tops between
    YEHUDIT and RICHARD, confronting them. It breaks into a full-
    on brawl between all five of them. This extended moment is
    like Jacob wrestling with his angel, like war.

The pithy music gets louder and louder to cover this shit show. The fight topples onto the ground, over the beam, and almost into the audience.

MARGARET: Stop stop stop STOP STOP STOP STOP STOP!!!

Finally everyone stops, spent and sprawled on the ground. The women break into laughter.

RICHARD: It's not funny.

Slowly they realize that LIZ's laughter has turned to tears. She is sobbing, head down, sound ripping out of her. The others try to comfort her. Finally, she sits on the beam.

LIZ: I did want to win.

MARYAM: What?

LIZ: I want . . . I want god *off* me, excised, removed, sucked out of memory, of marrow, of our psyche, our cells.

(to MARYAM) You appeared out of nowhere. On fire. Holy.

(to YEHUDIT) Imagine if all this ancient poison was gone, or if it never existed to get inside us at all, love would be like nothing we can dream of.

(to audience) Imagine . . . if we all just let ourselves leap, and fall, and tumble and never land.

(to MARYAM) You don't have to do anything. You don't have to choose.

LIZ is standing on the beam, and as each person speaks they also stand or sit on the beam. They each appear to be floating, suspended. They are talking to the world, themselves, the audience, each other.

YEHUDIT joins LIZ on the precipice.

YEHUDIT: Oh, yes you do.

RICHARD rises, joining them, speaking to himself.

RICHARD: Choose something.

MARGARET climbs onto the precipice.

MARGARET: Do it. Just go for it. Make a *choice.*

MARYAM stands. Now all of them are on the verge of leaping . . .

MARYAM: I have.

Beat.

They all inhale . . .

Lights out.

End.

ACKNOWLEDGEMENTS

Special thanks to Colin Rivers, Tommie-Amber Pirie, Philippa Domville, Patricia Hamilton, Melee Hutton, Rebecca Auerbach, Tom Barnett, John Beal, Melissa Convery, Jacqueline Costa, David Jansen, Erica Kopyto, Janis Purdy, Eli Purdy-Flacks, Jonny Purdy-Flacks (Ephraim and Yitzhak), Paul Lampert, Rabbi Deborah Landsberg, Sarah Orensetin, Prim Pemberton, Alex Poch-Goldin, Courtney Pyke, Allison Roth, Mary Elizabeth Willcott, Mojtaba Yaraghi, 4th Line Theatre, Obsidian Theatre, Studio 180, Tarragon Theatre, Theatre Passe Muraille, the Watah School, all of the Buddies in Bad Times Theatre staff and crew, the Zoomer team, Playwrights Canada Press and the Playwrights Guild of Canada.

Diane Flacks acknowledges the generous support of the Ontario Arts Council and the Canada Council for the Arts.

Diane Flacks is a writer/actor. Her plays include *Bear With Me*; *Random Acts*; *Myth Me*; *Waiting Room*; *By a Thread*; *Gravity Calling*; *Luba, Simply, Luba* and *Theory of Relatives*, as well as *SIBS* and *Care* with Richard Greenblatt. Diane also writes extensively for TV (among others, *Working the Engels*, *Workin' Moms*, *Baroness von Sketch Show*, *Qanurli* and *Kids in the Hall*). She has been the national parenting columnist for CBC Radio, and a contributor to *DNTO* and *Tapestry*. She was a feature columnist for the *Toronto Star* and the *Globe and Mail*. Diane has performed comedy everywhere from New York's Town Hall to local bars to the Winnipeg Comedy Festival. Her four solo shows have toured nationally and internationally. She is currently developing a one-person play called *Guilt* and a play with the Stratford Festival called *Blessed*. She has numerous acting credits over twenty-five years in the business, and in 2019 she played Nathan in *Nathan the Wise* at Stratford.

First edition: September 2019
Printed and bound in Canada by Rapido Books, Montreal

Jacket design by Kisscut Design
Cover photo © onemorenametoremember / photocase.com
Author photo © Tommie-Amber Pirie

 **PLAYWRIGHTS
CANADA PRESS**
202-269 Richmond St. W.
Toronto, ON
M5V 1X1

416.703.0013
info@playwrightscanada.com
www.playwrightscanada.com
@playcanpress